spot

BACKYARD ANIMALS

FROGS

by Marysa Storm

AMICUS | AMICUS INK

skin

legs

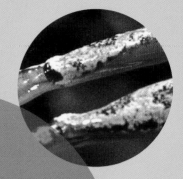

Look for these words and pictures as you read.

eye

vocal sac

Ribbit!
A frog is nearby.
Can you see it?

Some frogs are big.
Some are small.
They live everywhere
but Antarctica.

Look at the frog's skin.
It is smooth. It is moist.

skin

Look at the frog's vocal sac.
It helps male frogs call.
Croak!

vocal sac

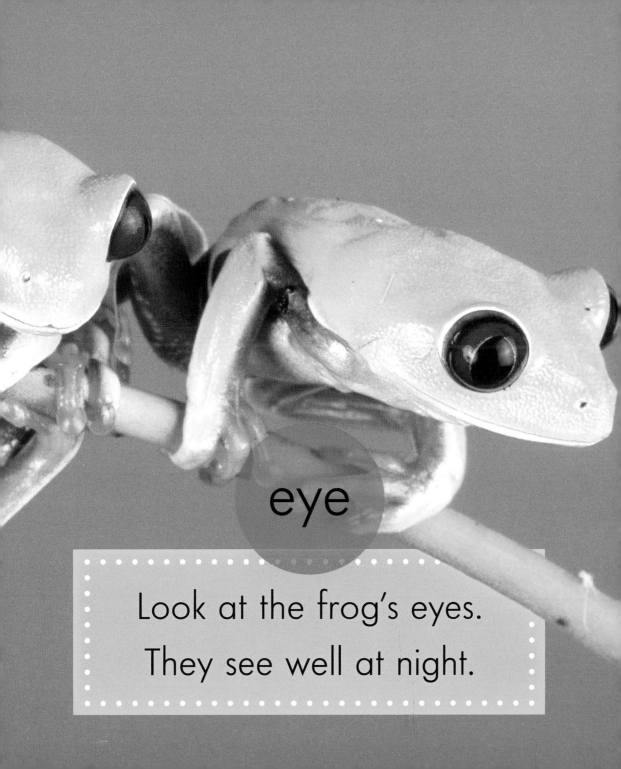

eye

Look at the frog's eyes.
They see well at night.

Look at the frog's legs.
They are long and strong.
Watch them leap!

legs

A frog looks for dinner.
The frog has a sticky tongue.
It will catch the bug.

Look at the frog's skin.
It is smooth. It is moist.

skin

Look at the frog's legs.
They are long and strong.
Watch them leap!

legs

skin

legs

Did you find?

eye

vocal sac

eye

Look at the frog's eyes.
They see well at night.

Look at the frog's vocal sac.
It helps male frogs call.
Croak!

vocal sac

Spot is published by Amicus and Amicus Ink
P.O. Box 1329, Mankato, MN 56002
www.amicuspublishing.us

Library of Congress Cataloging-in-Publication Data
Names: Storm, Marysa, author.
Title: Frogs / by Marysa Storm.
Description: Mankato, Minnesota : Amicus, 2018. | Series:
  Spot. Backyard animals | Audience: Grades K to 3.
Identifiers: LCCN 2016044416 (print) | LCCN 2017000696
  (ebook) | ISBN 9781681510910 (library binding) | ISBN
  9781681511818 (e-books) | ISBN 9781681522166 (pbk.)
Subjects: LCSH: Frogs--Juvenile literature.
Classification: LCC QL668.E2 S845 2018 (print) | LCC
  QL668.E2 (ebook) | DDC 597.8/9--dc23
LC record available at https://lccn.loc.gov/2016044416

Printed in the United States of America

HC 10 9 8 7 6 5 4 3 2 1
PB 10 9 8 7 6 5 4 3 2 1

Rebecca Glaser, editor
Deb Miner, series designer
Ciara Beitlich, book designer
Holly Young, photo researcher

Photos by Age Fotostock 2,
8–9, 10–11, 15; Alamy cover,
16; Dreamstime 1; iStock, 4–5;
Shutterstock 2, 3, 6–7, 15;
SuperStock 2, 12–13, 14, 15

FROGS